# THE CHECKLIST CHALLENGE GUIDE TO ✓ LIFE SKILLS

BY STEPHANIE PETERS

Raintree is an imprint of Capstone Global Library Limited, a company incorporated in England and Wales having its registered office at 264 Banbury Road, Oxford, OX2 7DY – Registered company number: 6695582

www.raintree.co.uk
myorders@raintree.co.uk

Text © Capstone Global Library Limited 2024
Paperback edition published in 2025

The moral rights of the proprietor have been asserted. All rights reserved. No part of this publication may be reproduced in any form or by any means (including photocopying or storing it in any medium by electronic means and whether or not transiently or incidentally to some other use of this publication) without the written permission of the copyright owner, except in accordance with the provisions of the Copyright, Designs and Patents Act 1988 or under the terms of a licence issued by the Copyright Licensing Agency, 5th Floor, Shackleton House, 4 Battle Bridge Lane, London, SE1 2HX (www.cla.co.uk). Applications for the copyright owner's written permission should be addressed to the publisher.

**Editorial Credits**
Editor: Donald Lemke; Designer: Kay Fraser; Media Researchers: Jo Miller and Svetlana Zhurkin; Production Specialist: Katy LaVigne

ISBN 978 1 3982 5212 7 (hardback)
ISBN 978 1 3982 5217 2 (paperback)

**British Library Cataloguing in Publication Data**
A full catalogue record for this book is available from the British Library.

**Image credits**
Getty Images: ajkkafe, cover (bottom right), Alistair Berg, 8, Alys Tomlinson, 14, gahsoon, 27, Jose Luis Pelaez Inc, 6, 24, 26, Lucy Lambriex, 29, Maskot, 17, PhotoAlto/Eric Audras, 16, RF Pictures, 21, SDI Productions, 25; Shutterstock: Ann in the uk, 15, Inside Creative House, 10, Krakenimages.com, 12, Monkey Business Images, cover (bottom left), 4, 7, 18, 22, New Africa, 23, otnaydur, 9, pixelheadphoto digitalskillet, 19, Plateresca, 28, Prostock-studio, cover (right), Sergey Novikov, 20, silverblackstock, 11, Suzanne Tucker, 13, Tatiana Gladskikh, 5

Every effort has been made to contact copyright holders of material reproduced in this book. Any omissions will be rectified in subsequent printings if notice is given to the publisher.

All the internet addresses (URLs) given in this book were valid at the time of going to press. However, due to the dynamic nature of the internet, some addresses may have changed, or sites may have changed or ceased to exist since publication. While the author and publisher regret any inconvenience this may cause readers, no responsibility for any such changes can be accepted by either the author or the publisher.

# CONTENTS

LEARNING LIFE SKILLS ............ 4

SPEAK UP AND BE HEARD ............ 6

MONEY MATTERS ............ 12

TAKE CARE, NOW ............ 18

SPREAD YOUR WINGS ............ 22

WANT TO TRY MORE? ............ 28

GLOSSARY ............ 30

FIND OUT MORE ............ 31

INDEX ............ 32

ABOUT THE AUTHOR ............ 32

Words in **bold** appear in the glossary.

# ☑ LEARNING LIFE SKILLS

Life can be hard work sometimes! Learning to face everyday challenges is a skill. A checklist can help you tackle these challenges head-on.

Are you ready to take the checklist challenge? The advice in this book will guide you towards creating your best life.

# ✓ SPEAK UP AND BE HEARD

You use your voice to talk. But are you using it to **communicate**? Good communication is key to getting along with others. It's a skill worth working on!

# CAN I SAY SOMETHING?

Who's taking out the rubbish tonight? Where are we going on holiday? Families make decisions like these every day. Your opinion matters. Add your voice to the **conversation**! Making sure you are heard is a skill for life.

# LEAD THE WAY

Being a leader is an important life skill and checklist item. Group activities often go better with someone in charge. A good leader **inspires** a group to do its best. They **motivate** group members towards a goal.

## MAY I HAVE YOUR ATTENTION, PLEASE?

Do you get **stage fright** at the thought of giving a speech? You're not alone. Public speaking scares a lot of people. Finding the confidence to address a crowd is a useful life skill.

**FACT:** The fear of public speaking is called glossophobia.

# ☑ MONEY MATTERS

Money is a big part of our lives. Knowing how to handle your own money is a checklist life skill everyone can use!

# MAKE SOME

Buying the things we need or want takes money. If there's something special you want, you could ask an adult to pay for it. Or you could earn the money yourself!

Making money is an important skill. It's also rewarding, especially if you earn it doing something you like.

## SAVE SOME

Spending money is fun. But it's good to get in the **habit** of saving too. That way, you'll have cash for big-ticket items, like a visit to an amusement park. Putting money aside to spend later on is a life skill you'll be glad you mastered.

# ACTIVITY: MONEY JARS

Want to see your savings grow? Plant your earnings in money jars. Find glass or plastic containers. (Recycled pasta sauce jars work well!) Label the jars *pennies*, *pounds* and *notes*. If you're saving up for something specific, add another label with that item's name on it. Keep adding to the jars. In time, your savings will bloom!

## BORROW AND LEND

At some point, you might need to **borrow** money from someone. Make sure you both agree that the money will be paid back. Decide when the paying back will happen. That way, you'll both feel okay with the **loan**. You'll also gain experience handling money.

# ☑ TAKE CARE, NOW

When you were little, your parents or carers looked after you. Now that you're older, you can start looking after yourself and those around you. Learning responsibility can be a great addition to any checklist.

# GIVE YOURSELF A BREAK

With school, homework and other activities, life can get busy. It's easy to feel **overwhelmed**. If that happens, talk to an adult. Together, you can work out how to take breaks when needed.

# SHARE THE CARE

Looking after a pet, plant or younger sibling is a long-lasting skill. It shows others that you're trustworthy and kind. It also proves that the **wellbeing** of others is important to you.

# ✓ SPREAD YOUR WINGS

The older you get, the more chances you'll have to explore your place in the world. Understanding your interests can help shape your life journey.

## YOU WON'T KNOW UNTIL YOU TRY!

New activities can be scary. It can be easy to steer clear of something if you think you won't be any good at it. But no one starts out perfect at anything! Accepting that you'll make mistakes is a valuable life skill.

# SOMEONE ELSE'S SHOES

People from all walks of life face difficulties every day. No one person can fix every problem. But you can take steps to make a positive impact. Getting involved with giving back to others is a life skill worth having. Add it to your checklist.

# ACTIVITY: CHARITY SALE

Do you have a cause you want to support? Consider having a sale for charity, where people donate their items to be sold. All money raised will go towards your chosen charity. It takes time and energy to organize this, so make sure you have plenty of both before going ahead.

**FACT:**
People gave £10.7 billion to charity in the UK in 2021.

# A PROBLEM? NO PROBLEM!

One day, you'll have your first job. Many employers look for people who can think on their feet to solve problems. You can practise that life skill now. Then you'll be ready when job opportunities come your way!

# WANT TO TRY MORE?

You've got all the important life skills checklist items! Now it's time to add some fun activities and experiences to your must-do list. Check out (and then check off) a few of these ideas.

- ☑ Ask an adult to teach you how to do your own laundry.

- ☑ Learn yoga poses by taking a class or following online instructions.

- ☑ Make your own soap by melting chopped-up blocks of glycerin in the microwave. Mix in coloured dye and fragrance oils, pour the mixture into moulds and chill until hardened.

☑ Play the sticky-note game with friends and family.
Ask yes-or-no questions to guess the person, place or thing written on the note stuck to your forehead.

☑ Create cheerful greetings cards to give to family and friends.

☑ Volunteer to help out at your local food bank.

☑ Interview adults to learn more about their jobs.

☑ Help out with a youth sports team.

# GLOSSARY

**borrow** use or have something that belongs to someone else for a while, with permission

**communicate** share facts, ideas or feelings with other people

**conversation** talk and listen with someone for a while

**habit** something that one does regularly, often without thinking about it

**inspire** fill someone with an emotion, idea or an attitude

**loan** money that is borrowed with a plan to pay it back

**motivate** encourage someone to do something

**overwhelm** have a very strong effect

**stage fright** nervousness people feel before appearing in front of an audience

**wellbeing** being happy and healthy, both mentally and physically

# FIND OUT MORE

## BOOKS

*Be Confident Be You*, Becky Goddard-Hill (Collins, 2023)

*Life Skills for Tweens* (Essential Life Skills for Teens), Ferne Bowe (Bemberton, 2023)

*You Are a Champion: How to Be the Best You Can Be*, Marcus Rashford (MacMillan, 2021)

## WEBSITES

**www.bbc.co.uk/teach/moodboosters**
Watch the videos on the BBC Moodboosters web page to help you tackle life's challenges.

**www.explorelearning.co.uk/free-resources/self-care-for-children-wellbeing-tips-explore-learning/**
This website has lots of advice on self-care and wellbeing.

# INDEX

activities 9, 19, 23

communication 6–7
confidence 10

decision-making 7

goals 9

habits 14
homework 19

jobs 13, 26

leadership 9
loans 16

money 12–14, 15, 16

pets 20
public speaking 10

responsibility 18

stage fright 10
stress 19

## ABOUT THE AUTHOR

Stephanie Peters has been writing books for young readers for more than 25 years. Among her most recent titles are *Sleeping Beauty: Magic Master* and *Johnny Slimeseed*, both for Raintree's Far-Out Fairy Tales and Folk Tales series. An avid reader, workout enthusiast and beach wanderer, Stephanie enjoys spending time with her children, Jackson and Chloe, her husband, Dan, and the family's two cats and two rabbits. She lives and works in Mansfield, Massachusetts, USA.